The Grumpy Millionaire

Written by John Parsons

Illustrated by Kerry Gemmill

Contents	Page
Chapter 1. *Entering the old house*	4
Chapter 2. *An angry old man*	10
Chapter 3. *The house is transformed*	17
Chapter 4. *Another transformation*	21
Chapter 5. *The most valuable painting*	26
Verse	32

The Grumpy Millionaire

With these characters . . .

Thomas Grabalott

Mitch Harrison

"He emptied his tin of dollar

Setting the scene . . .

Mitch Harrison couldn't think of a worse place to lose the softball. That stupid Daniel Smith had hit the ball so hard it had flown over the fence and smashed a window of the *old house*.

Little does Mitch know that someone lives in the old house and he is not happy about having his window broken. That someone is Thomas Grabalott, a lonely, grumpy millionaire who is about to learn a very valuable lesson.

:oins and started counting."

Chapter 1.

"NO TRESPASSING," read an old sign painted in straggly letters. The path rising in front of Mitch Harrison was cracked and overgrown. Huge, thorny blackberry bushes bulged out from either side. Slippery green moss covered the concrete, and ragged, drooping dandelions forced their way up and out of the cracks. Mitch couldn't think of a worse place to lose the softball. If only that stupid Daniel Smith hadn't hit it so hard, up and over the fence. If only that stupid Daniel Smith had hit it in the other direction, away from the old house ...

Mitch and his softball team had been practicing on the vacant lot next to the old house. Even though their bats, mitts, and masks were almost falling apart, *some* people still managed to belt the ball far too hard. Mitch wondered why it was always *his* job to retrieve the ball.

As Mitch crept up the path, thick blackberry thorns caught in his clothes and scratched his skin. He turned a corner and there it was, looming in front of him: the old house!

It looked hundreds of years old. The paint was peeling. Faded curtains were drawn across the dark, dirty windows. A silent black crow sat on one of the rusting gutters, watching him closely. Mitch shivered and took a deep breath. With a feeling of terror, he realized the broken glass meant he would have to go *inside* the old house to hunt for his softball.

Slowly, Mitch pushed his way through the overgrown plants to the darker side of the old house.

Towering trees blocked the sun from that side of the house. Mitch stooped to avoid their low branches as he moved closer.

Mitch started to wonder if the old softball was really worth it. Another hard whack and the ball would probably fall apart, anyway. Perhaps he should return to the team and say he couldn't find it.

Suddenly, Mitch gasped as he sensed a movement out of the corner of his eye. He turned his head and breathed a sigh of relief. It was only his reflection in a dark pane of glass set low in the wall. Next to the window was a small door. It was slightly open.

Taking a deep breath, Mitch slowly pushed open the door and stepped inside.

Inside, the room was dark, and the air had an old, dusty smell. Terrified, Mitch felt his way around the small room and into a long hallway. He couldn't see how high the ceiling was, but through the gloom he could see dozens of paintings on the wall. He peered closer. They were huge, gold-framed paintings.

Halfway down the hall, a grand staircase curled its way up into the darkness. Mitch crept down the hallway and stopped at the bottom of the staircase. On the wall next to the staircase was another painting. But this one was different. The picture was turned toward the wall, and he could see only the back of the frame. Mitch wondered why anyone would hang a picture backwards.

Too late, he heard something behind him!

Then, without warning, a cold, bony hand seized Mitch's shoulder.

"TRESPASSER!" came an old, rasping voice. Mitch was too terrified to turn around.

"What are you doing in my house?"

"I ... I ... ," stammered Mitch in terror.

"Did *you* break my window?" demanded the voice. "You will have to pay for that!"

"I'm very sorry," said Mitch, shaking like a leaf. "We didn't mean to do any damage."

The bony hand released its grip, and Mitch slowly turned around.

Chapter 2.

Standing in the hallway was an ancient-looking man hunched over and glaring. His face was dark and wrinkled, and his eyes were half-hidden under terrifying, bushy eyebrows.

"The softball team will pay for your broken window," said Mitch in a quivering voice.

"I don't want your money," growled the old man. "I am a millionaire! My name is Thomas Grabalott. I once owned all this land around here—all of it, right down to the sea. I sold it for millions of dollars. So I don't want your money. You can *work* for me instead."

Mitch knew he was trapped. His friends on the softball team wouldn't come to rescue him. They would think he had snuck home without finding the ball. There was nothing he could do, so he just nodded. His knees felt weak.

"I noticed you looking at my valuable art collection," said Mr. Grabalott, waving a shaky hand towards the paintings in the hall. "So you can work on them to repay me for my broken window. The frames need to be polished until the gold gleams again. And you won't be leaving until they're all done. All twenty of them!"

Mr. Grabalott disappeared into the small room Mitch had entered first. He emerged with an old rag and a bottle of polish.

"What's your phone number? I'll call your parents and tell them what you're doing. And then I'll be back to check up on you. So don't even think about taking short cuts. I want you to do a thorough job!"

After an hour, Mitch forgot about grumpy old Grabalott watching his every move from the bottom of the staircase. Although his arms were aching and tired from polishing, Mitch was fascinated by the paintings. They all looked expensive.

Some were of flowers and fruit while others were of important-looking ladies and gentlemen. There were scenes of old buildings and cities, rivers, and country landscapes. The paint on some of them was cracked with age, and others seemed as bright as the day they were painted.

But of all the paintings, Mitch was most curious about the painting hung backwards, which was hidden from view at the bottom of the stairs.

"They're worth hundreds and thousands of dollars," said Mr. Grabalott gruffly.

"They're very beautiful," said Mitch.

"Beautiful?" replied Mr. Grabalott. "Yes, I suppose they are," he said.

"Art is one of my favorite subjects at school," said Mitch. "These colors are amazing!"

Mr. Grabalott closed his eyes and thought of the gleaming, glittering piles of shiny coins that the paintings were worth. "Amazing," he agreed.

"But why is that one turned around?" asked Mitch, pointing to the painting at the bottom of the stairs.

"That's none of your business," said Mr. Grabalott with a snort. "Now, finish polishing those frames. I asked your mother if you could work until four o'clock, and you have only one hour left to finish the job."

Finally, Mitch finished polishing the frame on the last painting. He screwed the top back on the bottle of polish and walked over to the staircase, where the old man was hunched over with his arms folded.

"You should open up your house to let people see these paintings, Mr. Grabalott," suggested Mitch politely.

"People?" snorted Mr. Grabalott. "Why would I want to allow *people* into my house?"

"You might enjoy showing off your paintings," replied Mitch.

"I doubt it," replied Mr. Grabalott grumpily. "All people want to do is take my money ... *and* break my windows," he added, scowling at Mitch.

"You could charge each person a quarter to see the paintings," suggested Mitch.

The old man opened his eyes wide and scratched his chin. He thought for a moment.

"Now, THAT is a good idea!" Mr. Grabalott said. He narrowed his eyes and smiled at the thought of hundreds of people paying a quarter each just to look at his paintings. It was a very good idea! Even though he didn't need any more money, he *liked* the idea of making money for doing nothing.

Mitch sat down on the bottom step and stared at the hallway, deep in thought.

"You'd need to clean the hallway and brush away all the dust and cobwebs," he said.

But Mr. Grabalott's mind was somewhere else. He was thinking about his favorite subject—money!

"That's a good idea. So I'll expect you and your softball teammates at nine o'clock tomorrow morning, ready to start work!"

Mitch looked surprised. "But . . ."

"Tell them to let their parents know they have a job to do. Nine o'clock—and don't be late!" warned the old man.

He glared at Mitch, who decided not to argue.

Chapter 3.

"But what about our softball practice?" protested Daniel Smith when Mitch told the team about old Grabalott's plan. "We always have softball practice at nine o'clock on Sundays."

The rest of the team nodded in agreement. Everyone was scared at the thought of having to work in the old house.

"No softball practice tomorrow," said Mitch glumly. "Or else we'll all be in big trouble."

Reluctantly, everyone met at nine o'clock the next morning. Mitch led the way up the overgrown path to the house. No one said a word. Their eyes darted from side to side. The old house looked very scary.

Just as Mitch was about to knock on the front door, it swung open and Mr. Grabalott stood before the team.

"So, *you* are the hooligans who broke my window!" he growled at them all. "It's lucky there are so many of you, because there's a LOT of work to be done."

Mr. Grabalott led them inside the house and started bellowing orders.

"You! Get yourself a broom. You! Take this feather duster. You! Here's the vacuum cleaner."

Everyone did as they were told. As Mr. Grabalott hobbled around the house, he issued more orders. The curtains were flung open and the sun streamed in. Clouds of dust and cobwebs disappeared into the vacuum. Once more, the paintings in the hallway were dusted and the crooked ones were straightened. The path leading to the front door was swept clear of dirt and leaves.

Mr. Grabalott called over to Mitch. "Take this," he ordered, handing Mitch a sheet of paper and some coins. "Go photocopy twenty copies. Then stick them up in shop windows. I want hundreds of dollars ... I mean, *people* ... to come to my art exhibition."

Mitch was glad to leave the house. He raced down to the library and photocopied the sheet.

"EXHIBITION," it said. "An exhibition of valuable paintings owned by Mr. Grabalott will be held at his house next Saturday, September 24. Time: 9:00 A.M. to 5:00 P.M. Admission: 25¢."

At the end, in big letters, it said: "NO DISCOUNTS!"

By the time Mitch had photocopied the advertisements and stuck them in twenty shop windows, an hour had passed. Reluctantly, he made his way back to Mr. Grabalott's house. When he reached the house, he couldn't believe his eyes!

"This is amazing!" Mitch said, admiring the clean and tidy hallway. It didn't look anything like the old house he had crept into yesterday. Paintings gleamed and glittered on the walls. The carpets were full of color. Every trace of cobwebs and dust had vanished.

"I can't believe this is the same house," said Mitch enthusiastically.

"I can," groaned Daniel Smith. "I'm exhausted." The whole team looked tired. This was much harder work than softball practice!

Chapter 4.

The day of the exhibition arrived quickly. Mitch raced up the path to Mr. Grabalott's house. He wanted to see how many people would turn up. He wondered if they would like Mr. Grabalott's valuable art collection.

At first, Mitch didn't recognize the man standing on the doorstep. He was smartly dressed in a suit, a white shirt, and a dark red tie. His shoes were shining in the sunlight. But there was no mistaking that scowl.

"That will be one quarter," he said, frowning at Mitch.

"But ...," said Mitch.

"One quarter," repeated Mr. Grabalott. "NO DISCOUNTS!"

Mitch sighed and handed over a quarter. As he walked into the hallway, he noticed that the backwards painting was still hidden from view. Very soon, Daniel Smith and his parents arrived. Then, some more of his softball team mates lined up to pay their quarters. Before long, lots of people who had seen the advertisements in the shop windows were admiring Mr. Grabalott's paintings, too.

At first, Mr. Grabalott said only one thing to the visitors: "That will be one quarter." But soon, people started asking him questions about his paintings. They asked him what they represented or where he had bought them. Mr. Grabalott proudly told them how little he had paid for them and how much more the paintings were worth today.

"The longer I keep them, the more valuable they become," he said, wiggling his bushy eyebrows with pride.

Gradually, he even started to enjoy talking to the people who visited his home.

Mitch was amazed to hear him start saying "*Welcome* to my home. That will be one quarter." From Mr. Grabalott, that was really amazing to hear!

By the middle of the afternoon, Mr. Grabalott seemed to stand taller and straighter. His face appeared less wrinkled, and his eyebrows looked less terrifying. He smiled at the people who were admiring his art collection. He shook hands with them as they left and greeted new visitors with a wink and a smile.

"How nice to see you," he would say. "Welcome to my home. I hope you enjoy the paintings." Sometimes, he even forgot to ask for the quarter. But not very often.

A reporter from the local newspaper came to take some photographs of Mr. Grabalott standing by his paintings. She interviewed Mr. Grabalott so she could write an article about Mr. Grabalott's art collection.

"I'm quite enjoying myself," whispered Mr. Grabalott to Mitch. "I'd forgotten how nice it is to have people around."

Toward the end of the afternoon, Mr. Grabalott had cheered up so much that Mitch thought he would give people their quarters back. But, of course, he didn't. He placed all the quarters in a dented old tin he kept hidden in a kitchen cupboard.

The art exhibition was a great success. Everyone left the house talking about the wonderful paintings. They all smiled at Mr. Grabalott and thanked him for letting them into his home. He smiled back and waved goodbye. As the last person left, he even looked a little sad.

Then, Mr. Grabalott seemed to grow smaller and more hunched over again. He closed the door and shuffled into the kitchen. He tipped over his tin and began counting his quarters.

Chapter 5.

The Saturday after the art exhibition, Mitch, Daniel and the rest of the team were playing softball again in the empty lot next to the Grabalott house. Mitch cringed as Daniel Smith took a huge swing at the softball. But instead of hitting the softball towards Mr. Grabalott's house, the bat broke. The whole team groaned. Daniel stared at the broken bat.

"I guess that's the end of the softball team," he said. Everyone looked glum. They had only one bat, and Daniel Smith had broken it. What was worse, they had no money to buy another one.

As they gathered around the broken bat to see if it could be fixed, everyone was startled by a shout.

"Hey, you!"

Mitch turned in the direction of the voice. Mr. Grabalott was calling from an open window at the top of his house.

"Yes, you! Come on over." He was pointing at Mitch.

Mitch grimaced. What had he done now? He left the rest of the team and trudged up the path.

"I'm sorry," said Mr. Grabalott, when Mitch arrived at the front door. "After all your hard work, I don't even know your name."

"Mitch," said Mitch. He was surprised by Mr. Grabalott's friendly tone.

"I have something to show you, Mitch," said Mr. Grabalott. Mitch followed him inside.

"I know you were curious about this painting," said Mr. Grabalott. "So I wanted you to be the first to see it."

He pointed to the backwards painting at the bottom of the stairs. It had been turned around. Mitch gasped.

It was the most beautiful painting he had ever seen. It was an oil painting of a group of laughing children playing at the beach. The children wore old-fashioned bathing suits. An older woman, dressed in old-fashioned clothes watched over them.

Mitch stared at the painting, imagining their shouts and screams of laughter as they played in the sand.

Mitch walked up to the painting to take a closer look. On the bottom of the frame was a tiny brass label.

"Harriet G., Louisa G., and Thomas G., with their mother. Pebble Beach, 1918," he read.

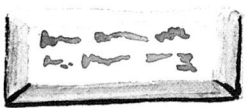

Suddenly, Mitch understood who the people in the painting were.

"This really is your most valuable painting, isn't it, Mr. Grabalott?" asked Mitch.

Mr. Grabalott smiled at Mitch and then looked up at the painting. For a moment, he looked sad, but then the smile returned to his face even bigger and brighter than before.

"Yes, Mitch, it is my most valuable painting. But it took you to remind me that the most valuable things are not always those that cost the most."

Mitch looked at Mr. Grabalott. Somehow, he seemed very different from the man he had first seen hidden in the darkness of the old house.

"I met many nice people last Saturday," Mr. Grabalott said. "It can be lonely living in this big old house. Sometimes, at my age, you don't want to be reminded of the times when you were happy and carefree." He nodded at the painting. "But I want to thank you for reminding me that all these paintings are really worth nothing if no one can enjoy them."

He asked Mitch to join him in the small room off the hallway Mitch had first seen when he had crept into the house.

Mitch followed Mr. Grabalott into the room and couldn't help noticing a huge box on the floor.

"Here is something to say *thank you*," said Mr. Grabalott. "Please open it."

Mitch opened the box. What he saw left him speechless.

There were brand-new aluminum softball bats and shiny white leather balls. Eleven brand new softball mitts lay beside the balls. There was even a catcher's mask and some rubber mats to mark the bases.

"But, Mr. Grabalott, you shouldn't have bought these!" exclaimed Mitch. "These must have cost a fortune."

"No," said Mr. Grabalott, grinning. "They didn't cost *me* anything."

He winked.

"But they cost everybody else a quarter each!"

"The most valuable things ...

Being rich in an
Empty house
Affords little pleasure,
Unless you choose
To share your treasures
With young and old.